William G. Thompson

Successful brain grafting

William G. Thompson

Successful brain grafting

ISBN/EAN: 9783337873769

Printed in Europe, USA, Canada, Australia, Japan

Cover: Foto ©ninafisch / pixelio.de

More available books at **www.hansebooks.com**

*Reprinted from the New York Medical Journal
for June 28, 1890.*

SUCCESSFUL BRAIN GRAFTING.

By W. GILMAN THOMPSON, M. D.,

PROFESSOR OF PHYSIOLOGY IN THE NEW YORK UNIVERSITY MEDICAL COLLEGE ;
VISITING PHYSICIAN TO THE PRESBYTERIAN AND THE NEW YORK HOSPITALS.

ATTEMPTS have been made to graft nearly all the different tissues of the body. Skin, bone, teeth, muscle, nerves, glands, eyes, mucous membrane, etc., have all been grafted with more or less success, but successful brain grafting has not heretofore been performed. With the exception of skin grafting, and possibly mucous-membrane grafting, the results of such experiments have been of little practical value. They are, however, of great scientific interest in demonstrating the relative vitality of different tissues and the histological changes which accompany degenerative processes. The laws of atrophy and final disappearance of disused organs, so ably advocated by Darwin, are equally striking with regard to individual tissues and cells, and it is a well-recognized fact that the higher the original development of a tissue or cell has been—i. e., the more it has been differentiated or specialized from the amœba type—the more profoundly is it affected by alterations in environment or nutrition, so as to degenerate completely, or be replaced by some form of tissue like the connective, which is of lower development but stronger vitality. The result of

SUCCESSFUL BRAIN GRAFTING.

nerve grafting and of nerve suture after complete section have varied greatly in the hands of different operators, but, despite many discouraging failures, there is no doubt that in man, as well as in the lower animals, nerve fibers may reunite when sutured even after secondary degeneration has occurred, and they exhibit restoration of function. For this to occur, however, the nerves must be in communication with some trophic center. Nerve grafting does not succeed so well as nerve sutures in favorable cases. It occurred to me recently, while studying cerebral localization in the lower animals, that it would be interesting to graft a piece of brain tissue from one side of a dog's brain to the other, or from one animal's brain into another's, and study its vitality. Of course, I had no expectation of being able to restore abolished function by the operation, but the question of vitality of the brain tissue and the course of its degeneration is a subject which is of very wide interest. The first experiments were preliminary, made in order to ascertain whether the transplanted brain would be immediately absorbed or would slough away.

Experiment I.—Two large dogs, A and B, were simultaneously trephined over the right occipital region; 8 c. c. of brain tissue were excised in one piece and exchanged; the piece from dog A was put into the opening in the brain of dog B, and *vice versa.* On the third day both dogs were killed, and the transplanted pieces of brain tissue looked normal, and in each case they were so adherent and firmly covered with fibrous exudation that it was impossible to pull them off with forceps without laceration. Total blindness of the eye opposite the lesion resulted in each dog, as was expected.

Experiment II.—A cat and a dog were simultaneously trephined, and 3·5 c. c. of brain tissue were removed from the dog's left occipital region and transplanted into an opening of the same size in the cat's left occipital region. Three days later the cat was killed. The transplanted dog's brain was found where it had been placed, firmly adherent to the cat's brain by a layer of fibrin, which varied from one fourth to half an inch in thickness. The cat was, of course, totally blind in the right eye.

Experiment III.—Another cat and dog were simultaneously trephined; 4 c. c. of brain tissue were excised from the dog's right occipital region and replaced by an equal quantity of cat's brain from the same region. On the fourth day the cat's brain was found adherent to the dog's by a layer of fibrin.

No microscopic examination was made in connection with these experiments, as it was intended only to determine the possibility of the transplanted tissue adhering. Being satisfied in regard to this matter, I secured a large dog and performed

Experiment IV.—A half-inch trephine was used and a button of bone was cut nearly through over the left occipital region, leaving a small attached margin so that the button could be elevated and then depressed like a little trap-door. Through the opening 2 c. c. of brain tissue were removed. A cat was simultaneously trephined and 1·5 c. c. of brain from her left occipital region were transferred in eight seconds to the opening in the dog's brain. The trephine opening was closed by the button, and the wound, which had been opened under careful antisepsis, was closed and dressed with layers of antiseptic gauze wet with thick collodion, which is the only practical dressing for brain operations on dogs, because they can not tear it off. The dog was totally blind for the eye opposite the lesion, and so remained until his death. He was, unfortunately, not tested as carefully in regard to the other eye. He was very dull—a street mongrel—and it did not occur to me to do more than test the vision of the eye opposite the lesion (which I have invariably found absent in such cases, with normal vision on the side of the lesion). As the autopsy showed, however, there was secondary degeneration of the opposite occipital region, which must have progressed far enough to have greatly impaired the

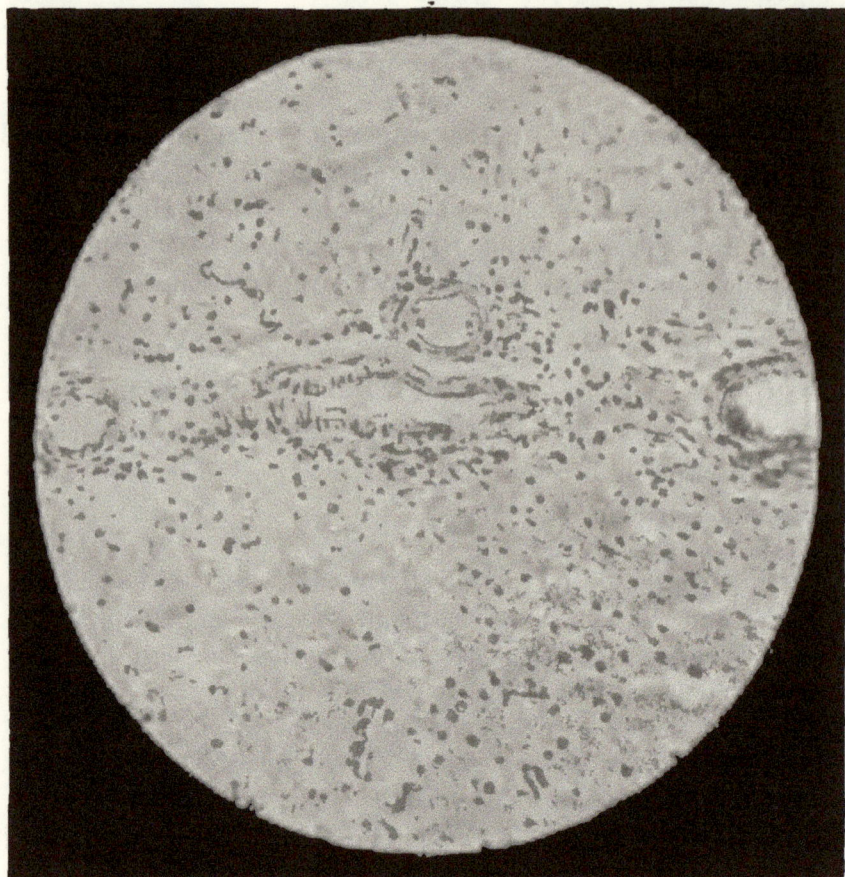

Micro-photograph of a brain graft. The upper half of the picture reproduces a
section through the cat's brain; the lower half, a section through the dog's
brain; the connective tissue uniting the two crosses the median line. Three
large blood-vessels are seen in transverse section, and one (in the center) in
longitudinal section. On the right center the line of union is very perfect,
there being a minimum of connective tissue here, and the two varieties of brain
seem fused together. On the left center, just above the line of union, a slight
tear was made in the cat's cortex in preparing the section; this was unavoidable,
in order to get the section thin enough for photographing. In all the other sections no such tear exists, and the line of union of the two brains is as perfect as
it is seen to be on the right of this photograph. The picture is not magnified to
show detail; it is merely intended to present the relative thickness of the line
of connective tissue and some of the larger nuclei and blood-vessels. (For this
photograph I am indebted to the kindness of Dr. H. S. Stearns, instructor in the
Pathological Department, and director of the Photographic Department of the
Loomis Laboratory.)

vision of the left eye. The dog made a good recovery from the operation, although he was very feeble for a few days and had to be fed by nutrient enemata. Subsequently he appeared normal in every way, excepting the loss of vision. He was killed at the end of seven weeks, when the piece of transplanted cat's brain was found firmly adherent to the dog's brain, with the pia mater intact. The brain was hardened in Müller's fluid for some weeks, and the following report of its examination has been kindly furnished me by Mr. Warren Coleman, assistant in the Physiological Department of the Loomis Laboratory, who prepared specimens of the brain for microscopic demonstration:

"*Gross Examination.*—The cerebral hemispheres measure 5·2 ctm. in breadth, 5·5 ctm. in length, and 3·5 ctm. in depth. The cerebellum was 3·5 ctm. broad and 2·9 ctm. deep through the medulla. The portion of brain transplanted now measures 1·9 × 0·5 × 0·5 ctm. It was grafted into the middle of the second occipital gyrus, its long axis extending outward and backward and involving a small part of the third occipital gyrus. The surface of the brain over the transplanted portion was somewhat shrunken. At a corresponding point in the opposite (right) hemisphere there appeared to be degeneration extending somewhat farther forward.

"*Microscopical Examination.*—The whole of the transplanted tissue was removed, together with a surrounding zone of dog's brain. This tissue was imbedded in celloidin, and vertical sections were cut in various parts. The vitality of the transplanted tissue has been maintained throughout, except at its inner extremity; here degenerative changes are well marked. The cells in this region are shrunken and irregular in outline, the protoplasm is granular, and the nuclei either stain very badly or refuse to take up the stain at all. In other parts the cells are intact, but their outline is somewhat irregular. From the surface of union of the two brains lines of degeneration extend down into the dog's brain, along the margin of which are seen cells larger than those found elsewhere. Many of the cells observed show beginning atrophic changes; these might be due, however, to the hardening process. Their nuclei are situated eccentrically. Between the two kinds of brain tissue a narrow band of connective tissue has formed, which firmly unites the grafted cat's brain to the dog's throughout their entire contiguous surfaces. This is most marked at the middle and inner extremity, where it reaches the width of a dozen fibers. Along its line numerous blood vessels have developed, some of which are of considerable size. The transplanted cat's brain is covered with pia mater perfectly continuous with that over the dog's brain. This pia was transplanted together with the cat's brain. The vessels of the cat's pia are large and numerous; the pia itself is somewhat thickened.

"The examination of the corresponding portion of the opposite hemisphere of the dog's brain gives the following results: Degenerative changes here are very marked. A portion of the brain tissue and the pia covering it are entirely gone. The cells in the neighborhood are granular and their nuclei do not appropriate the stain. A little removed from the point of greatest degeneration the brain shows a reticulated structure from the absence of cells. Here there is extensive diapedesis of the red blood cells. In other parts of the section no red blood cells are to be seen, but the brain cells contain a deposit of brown granules, showing that the red blood cells had broken down with the formation of hæmatoidin. The vessels of this region are enlarged and actively congested.

"At no point am I able to trace any communicating nerve fibers or axis cylinders between the two varieties of brain tissue, although here and there the line of union of connective tissue appears so narrow as to make the two brains almost continuous in structure. While some of the cells of the cat's brain are completely degenerated, the majority of them are still quite distinct and in some the walls are yet visible. Many of them do not look at all different from any piece of cat brain tissue kept for some weeks in hardening solutions, as this one was."

The features of interest of this experiment are the facts that—

1. There is complete union, through organized connective tissue, of the contiguous portions of the two brains.

2. After seven weeks the cat's brain still maintained enough vitality to be distinctly recognized as brain tissue.

3. Brains of animals of two very different species were thus made to unite.

4. The cat and dog pias present perfect union as well.

5. There is a sympathetic degeneration of the corresponding convolutions upon the opposite side of the dog's brain. For this curious fact 1 can not account. I have never noticed it before, in as many as fifty operations upon this region of the brain of cats and dogs,* although 1 have sometimes seen removal of a part of the occipital region result in extensive softening of the entire hemisphere of the same side. The opposite degeneration in this case may possibly be a mere coincidence; if so, it is a very unusual and remarkable one. There was no meningitis to favor it.

6. There was descending secondary degeneration of the dog's brain on the side of the graft, as is usual in cases of simple excision of brain cortex; hence the cat's cortex had not succeeded in acting as a nutrient center for the dog's brain. (The microscopic specimens showing the line of union of the two brains were shown to several competent microscopists, who indorsed their appearance as herein described, so that there can be no question of the accuracy of the observation.)

* W. Gilman Thompson and Sanger Brown, Experiments upon the Cortical Sight Center. Researches of the Loomis Laboratory, No. 1, 1890, p. 13.

I think the main fact of this experiment—namely, that brain tissue has sufficient vitality to survive for seven weeks the operation of transplantation without wholly losing its identity as brain substance—suggests an interesting field for further research, and I have no doubt that other experimenters will be rewarded by investigating it.

49 EAST THIRTIETH STREET.